30 Days of Fox Medicine

Decoding Hidden Messages from Your Spirit Animal

Harnessing the Power and Wisdom of Fox Medicine

Diana Loera

Table of Contents

Other Books Available from Loera Publishing LLC

Our books are available in the USA and abroad via over 40,000+ retailers including local independent bookstores plus libraries, schools and universities.

30 Days of Otter Medicine

Decoding Hidden Messages from Your Spirit Animal Guide

ISBN – 978-1-958814-84-0

30 Days of Chakra Balancing: Your Own Personal Chakra Journey for Learning and Navigating the Chakric System for Love, Health, Wealth, and Happiness and More

ISBN 979-8-9852282-9-8

Rune Casting Workbook: Learning Guide for Reading Runes

ISBN 979-8985228236

Tarot Cards Coloring and Learning Workbook: Mastering Tarot Card Meaning and Symbols

ISBN 979-8985228243

Tarot Card Workbook Journal: A Personal Learning Tarot Card Workbook Journal for Understanding and Reading Tarot Cards.

ISBN 979-8985228229

New Titles Coming in 2022 – 2023!

30 Days of Bear Medicine

Decoding Hidden Messages from Your Spirit Animal Guide

30 Days of Dragonfly Medicine

Decoding Hidden Messages from Your Spirit Animal Guide

Fox Medicine is Calling

If you've picked up this book, most likely the Fox has been calling you lately.

Spirit Animal Medicine can be a very loud calling that vibrates through our soul or a soft whisper on a summer breeze.

Once we have attuned into a certain spirit animal guide, one needs to determine the reason for his or her appearance in our life.

Fox brings with him or her a reminder It teaches you the art of benevolence and how mentally responsive you should be when trying to escape tricky situations in life.

Fox comes to teach you how to maneuver events and deal with the people in your life. When going through challenging times in life, look closely at Fox. Fox medicine you the art of benevolence and how mentally responsive you should be when trying to escape tricky situations in life.

Fox symbolizes several things -

Cleverness

Independence

Playfulness and Mischievousness

Beauty

Protection

Good Luck

Why is Fox medicine calling you now? Or has it been calling for some time and today you realized it? It doesn't matter, what matters is you hear Fox speaking to you, offering help and guidance on your path.

Native American Culture and the Fox

In the Northeast, Midwest and Plains tribes, Fox is generally an animal spirit associated with intelligence and wisdom, who occasionally help people or animals to solve a problem or punishes somebody careless or arrogant.

A fox's spiritual presence is thought of as the best guide to someone's destined path.

Seeing a fox may also mean that you have a situation that needs to be solved. The fox spirit is known to guide you to a solution.

Is Fox Medicine Calling You?

Take a few minutes to reflect upon the questions in this chapter. There are no right or wrong answers, but your answers may give you some insight regarding why the Fox has come calling in your life.

Do you feel your energy levels are low? Why?

_____

_____

_____

_____

_____

_____

_____

Do you feel your mind is cloudy? Why?

_____

_____

_____

_____

_____

_____

_____

_____

_____

Are you ready for a time of transformation? Why?

_____

_____

_____

_____

_____

_____

_____

Do you feel disconnected – from yourself, nature, others? Why?

_____

_____

_____

_____

_____

_____

_____

_____

_____

Do you desire to be more playful? Why?

_____

_____

_____

_____

_____

_____

_____

_____

_____

Do you have a feeling of dread or difficulty in adapting to changes in your life? Why?

_____

_____

_____

_____

_____

_____

_____

_____

_____

Do you desire to hear your inner voice again? Why?

_____

_____

_____

_____

_____

_____

_____

_____

_____

Have you forgotten how to rely on your inner voice and/or senses? Why?

_____

_____

_____

_____

_____

_____

_____

_____

_____

Do you want to increase your intellect but just can't get started? Why?

_____

_____

_____

_____

_____

_____

_____

_____

_____

_____

Do you feel everything is out of your control lately? Why?

_____

_____

_____

_____

_____

_____

_____

_____

_____

Do you feel more and more stressed by things going on around you? Why?

_____

_____

_____

_____

_____

_____

_____

_____

_____

Have you forgotten the last time you laughed had fun and enjoyed life? Why?

_____

_____

_____

_____

_____

_____

_____

_____

_____

Does your life seem endlessly monotonous now? Why?

_____

_____

_____

_____

_____

_____

_____

_____

_____

Does the idea of some changes make you feel afraid and/or worried? Why?

_____

_____

_____

_____

_____

_____

_____

_____

_____

Do you want to be more eager to do things in your life? Why?

_____

_____

_____

_____

_____

_____

_____

_____

_____

Fox Medicine Affirmations

What are affirmations?

Affirmations are simple, positive statements you say, think, or write down multiple times a day.

You are stating a goal you want to accomplish in its completed state, which helps to change your mindset.

Below are some affirmations for Fox Medicine. In the workbook, you will be writing out your own affirmations daily. You can use the ones below, modify them or make your own unique ones – whatever suits you best.

I'm ready to change my life.

I choose to change my life one step at a time, and today I am making that step.

Change is a necessity, and I'm happy I am making it happen today.

Change is good. Change is wanted and needed. Change is happening as I speak/write these words.

I am happy following these changes as it leads me closer and closer to the person I wish to become.

To be who I want to be, I must make a change. Today I change my life.

Each day brings me new opportunities to change my life and make it the best life I deserve.

I start my day with self-acceptance and self-love as they change the way I look at myself.

I am grateful for all the changes in my life, as they have led me to this moment and made me who I am.

As I start this day, I attract positive changes and easily accept them in my life.

I am free to change my life whenever I want, and I choose to start today.

Today, I work on creating my best life.

Today I change myself.

Today I change my life.

Today, I choose to change my life through kindness, self-love, and self-compassion.

Every change I bring into my life makes me more content and happier than ever.

I am talented and capable of changing my life. I choose to start today.

I change my life, and I am doing it every day.

Every day brings me new and exciting changes that lead me to my best life.

Every change is a blessing, and I am excited to see all the opportunities and happy moments it brings me.

Dreaming of the Fox

If Fox comes to you in your dreams, he or she may be delivering a message from other realms. It may be time for personal freedom or taking time for yourself.

Fox shows you that happiness and comfort is not something you find outside of yourself, but within. The message may also be that material things are not necessary when looking for happiness and joy.

Fox may also be trying to show you that perhaps something in life is pulling you down to the point of drowning. There are ways to make changes in your life without becoming overwhelmed.

If Fox comes to you in a dream, it's time to assess whether something in life is pulling you down to the point of drowning. There is a way to meet change without letting it overwhelm. Adaptation and a positive mindset are the keys to success.

Fox may be the bearer of a message from other realms, often playful. It's time for personal liberation. Don't take things so seriously. Release your worries by getting back in touch with your inner child.

When the Fox in your dream is floating on its back, it represents acceptance. There are things you cannot change in your life. Accept where you can bring positive transformation, and where your limits lie.

The Fox is considered an omen of good luck, but it is sometimes associated with the fox and the same trickster-like characteristics of the fox. The latter correspondences might come through in a dream scenario and could mean you need to be more flexible, adaptable, and willing to bend in a situation in your waking life. It can also signify the need to get in touch with your feminine side.

The realm of the Fox is often the water where it loves to play and jump around: If you see the creature in your dreams as it plays in the water, diving deep into the watery depths, then the dream might be telling you it is time for you to dig deep when doing your emotional work.

Fox dreams may be telling you to enjoy some downtime while engaging in some imaginative, and creative ideas.

When Fox comes into your dreams, it may be reminding you that you can achieve a balance between work and play, and it hints at the fact that you should continue to nurture and nourish yourself.

The skill in which the Fox dives into the water and swims about is suggestive as well; your dream may be telling you that you will have no trouble whatsoever navigating through an emotional situation or that you will not feel as if you are drowning in emotions or problems.

When Fox dives deeply in the water, he or she may be telling you to take a closer look and examine below the surface of a matter.

Fox Medicine Message

The message that Fox brings is to play.

Whatever hurtful circumstance that came into your life, Fox's message is to dive under the trouble, let it roll on past while we twirl and play.

Having playtime is the best way to heal a wounded soul. When Fox medicine comes into your life, it is time to remember the glorious delight of having fun and playing.

What things do you find fun? rives in your life, it's time to reconnect your goals with the spirit of fun which compelled you to engage in those goals in the first place.

How do we keep life fun? Why do activities and relationships lose their enjoyment? And how do we get that enjoyment back? Fox medicine teaches us how to live a happy and joyful life.

Fox medicine is a fluid, flowing dance with the ever-changing days. Fox knows when to shift and when to hold ground.

Fox medicine is a calling to delve deep and develop your own sense of intuition.

Fox medicine tells you to listen to your senses and go with the currents of your emotions.

The more you trust yourself, the more trustworthy you become.

Fox medicine teaches us how to float through life and listen to our soft quiet inner voice.

It is that voice who will instruct us on how to move with perfect grace through a storm and land onto new shores without falling apart.

The Fox Spirit Animal Totem takes playtime very seriously. Having fun is the meaning of her life. In Fox's world all beings are playful until proven un-playful. Her medicine is a spontaneous celebration and an eagerness to applaud others. She offers lessons in collective cooperation. There is no leader in a holt of Foxs. Leadership in play time cycles through whichever team member has the most information for the next task at hand. All differences are welcome as fascinating curiosities and competition is viewed as two players playing their best game. This medicine teaches us to seek worthy playmates whose skills will improve our own. So serious is Fox's need to play that finding time for playing is like finding time for eating. Fun is a life imperative, not a luxury. If unhappiness has lodged itself into your life for more than a week, it is urgent that you go find something you enjoy. All the complications will sort themselves out when you turn off the brain and get in the water.

To do anything well, Fox knows she must open herself up to the experience completely and allow herself to be changed by the unpredictable forces of nature.

Foxs show us that being playful is a good thing. Being playful isn't the same as being naive.

Fox is fiercely protective. Cross a boundary, mess with her family and Fox's fierceness will come into a full roar.

If boundaries have been crossed and injury has been committed, a person with Fox medicine will not hesitate to show their fury and defend their integrity. They will often enjoy doing so as well, because Fox medicine people are always making whatever they do fun, even getting angry.

But anger is just another tide to be released. Holding grudges is hard to do when you live in the ocean.

Don't stay upset for too long. It just isn't fun.

Find a way to vent and release.

Enjoy life. Live each day to the fullest.

Fox Medicine Writing Prompts

Fox medicine reminds us to bring joy and play into our lives.

Next are a few writing prompts to help you with claiming Fox Medicine in your life. There are no right or wrong answers to these questions.

What's one thing you can do right now to be more connected to joy?

_____

_____

_____

_____

_____

_____

_____

_____

_____

_____

What are three words/phrases that come to mind when you think of joy?

_____

_____

_____

_____

_____

_____

_____

What kind of thoughts would Fox think about play and joy?

Write about a time in your life when you felt pure joy.

_____

_____

_____

_____

_____

_____

_____

_____

_____

_____

What upcoming situation could use a little joy? How can you bring joy into that experience?

_____

_____

_____

_____

_____

_____

_____

_____

Describe a time when you discovered joy where you didn't expect it.

Imagine one scene from your perfect day. Write about the scene that you see.

_____

_____

_____

_____

_____

_____

_____

_____

Beginning Your 30 Day Fox Medicine Journey

The next section of this book is your 30 Day Fox Medicine Journey. Each day you will have four pages – Daily Affirmations, Daily Guidance, Daily Messages and Daily Reflection.

There are no right or wrong answers.

Each day you will write out your affirmations – they may be the same daily or they may change.

This is the same for Daily Guidance, Daily Messages and Daily Reflection. Listen to your inner voice.

Tune in to Fox Medicine.

If you miss a day or don't feel that working on your workbook that day, just continue on when you're ready.

May your life be transformed by the wisdom and knowledge of Fox Medicine as you do your 30 Day Fox Medicine Journey.

30 DAYS OF
FOX MEDICINE

Come along and tune into Fox Medicine for 30 days.
Discover yourself on a personal life changing journey

YOUR NAME

30 DAYS OF FOX MEDICINE

Welcome to your Spirit Animal Journey. For the next 30 days, you'll attune into the powerful medicine and wisdom of Fox.

This is your own personal journey. Otter medicine has beckoned you/ There is no right or wrong answers, just follow the path of the messages and wisdom Fox reveals.

NOTES

NOTES

DAILY GUIDANCE

How does the fox spirit animal fit me?

_____
_____
_____
_____

What messages does the fox have for me?

_____
_____
_____
_____

What is the fox asking me to be aware of?

_____
_____
_____
_____

Thoughts   Feelings

_____   _____
_____   _____
_____   _____
_____   _____

DAILY FOX MESSAGES

Fox encourages creativity

Fox Messages

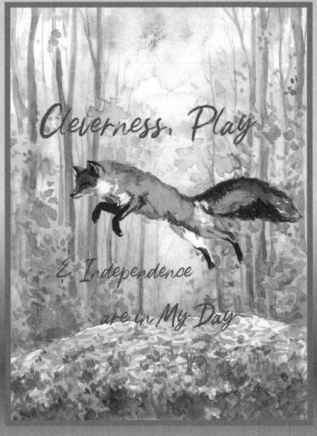

Cleverness, Play & Independence are in My Day

DAILY REFLECTION

_____
_____
_____
_____
_____
_____
_____
_____
_____
_____
_____
_____
_____
_____
_____
_____

DAILY FOX AFFIRMATIONS

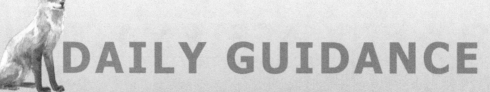

DAILY GUIDANCE

How does the fox spirit animal fit me?

_____
_____
_____
_____

What messages does the fox have for me?

_____
_____
_____
_____

What is the fox asking me to be aware of?

_____
_____
_____
_____

Thoughts   **Feelings**

_____   _____
_____   _____
_____   _____
_____   _____

DAILY FOX MESSAGES

Fox encourages creativity

Fox Messages

Cleverness, Play

& Independence

are in My Day

DAILY REFLECTION

_____

_____

_____

_____

_____

_____

_____

_____

_____

_____

_____

_____

_____

_____

_____

_____

_____

DAILY FOX AFFIRMATIONS

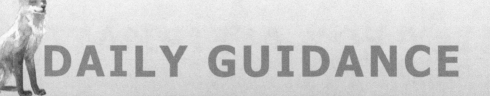

DAILY GUIDANCE

How does the fox spirit animal fit me?

_____
_____
_____
_____

What messages does the fox have for me?

_____
_____
_____
_____

What is the fox asking me to be aware of?

_____
_____
_____
_____

Thoughts	Feelings
_____	_____
_____	_____
_____	_____

DAILY FOX MESSAGES

Fox encourages creativity

Fox Messages

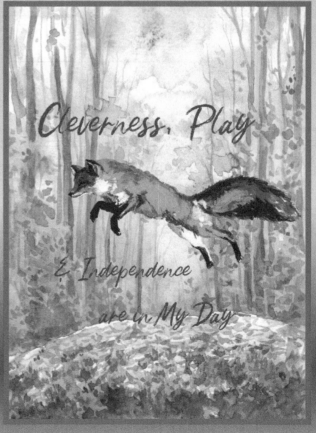

Cleverness, Play & Independence are in My Day

DAILY REFLECTION

_____
_____
_____
_____
_____
_____
_____
_____
_____
_____
_____
_____
_____
_____
_____
_____
_____
_____

DAILY FOX AFFIRMATIONS

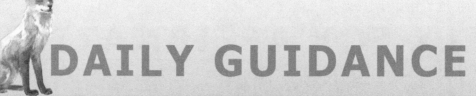

DAILY GUIDANCE

How does the fox spirit animal fit me?

_____
_____
_____
_____

What messages does the fox have for me?

_____
_____
_____
_____

What is the fox asking me to be aware of?

_____
_____
_____
_____

Thoughts   **Feelings**

_____   _____
_____   _____
_____   _____
_____   _____

DAILY FOX MESSAGES

Fox encourages creativity

Fox Messages

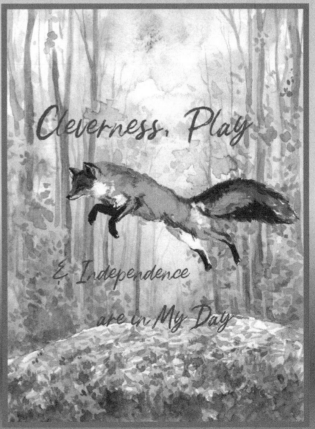

Cleverness, Play & Independence are in My Day

DAILY REFLECTION

DAILY FOX AFFIRMATIONS

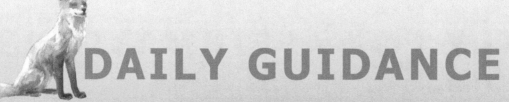

DAILY GUIDANCE

How does the fox spirit animal fit me?

_____

_____

_____

_____

What messages does the fox have for me?

_____

_____

_____

_____

What is the fox asking me to be aware of?

_____

_____

_____

_____

Thoughts	Feelings
_____	_____
_____	_____
_____	_____
_____	_____

DAILY FOX MESSAGES

Fox encourages creativity

Fox Messages

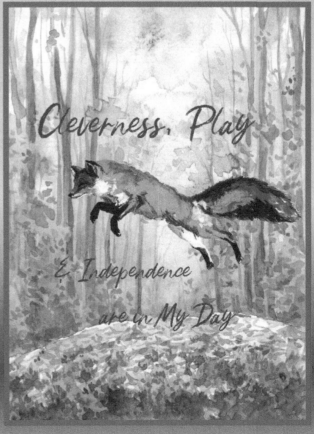

Cleverness, Play & Independence are in My Day

DAILY REFLECTION

_____

_____

_____

_____

_____

_____

_____

_____

_____

_____

_____

_____

_____

_____

_____

_____

_____

DAILY FOX AFFIRMATIONS

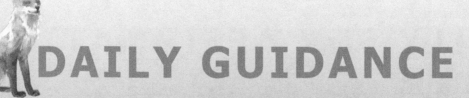

DAILY GUIDANCE

How does the fox spirit animal fit me?

_____
_____
_____
_____

What messages does the fox have for me?

_____
_____
_____
_____

What is the fox asking me to be aware of?

_____
_____
_____
_____

Thoughts   **Feelings**

_____   _____
_____   _____
_____   _____
_____   _____

DAILY FOX MESSAGES

Fox encourages creativity

Fox Messages

Cleverness, Play & Independence are in My Day

DAILY REFLECTION

DAILY FOX AFFIRMATIONS

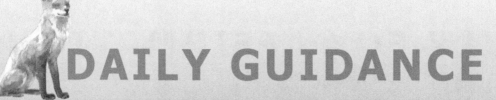

DAILY GUIDANCE

How does the fox spirit animal fit me?

_____
_____
_____
_____

What messages does the fox have for me?

_____
_____
_____
_____

What is the fox asking me to be aware of?

_____
_____
_____
_____

Thoughts   **Feelings**

_____   _____
_____   _____
_____   _____
_____   _____

DAILY FOX MESSAGES

Fox encourages creativity

Fox Messages

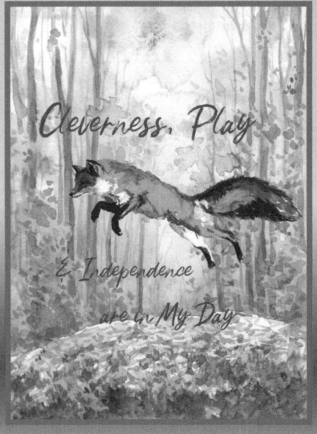

Cleverness, Play

& Independence

are in My Day

DAILY REFLECTION

_____
_____
_____
_____
_____
_____
_____
_____
_____
_____
_____
_____
_____
_____
_____
_____

DAILY FOX AFFIRMATIONS

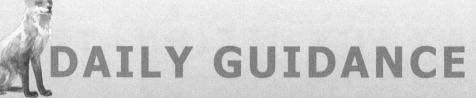

DAILY GUIDANCE

How does the fox spirit animal fit me?

_____
_____
_____
_____

What messages does the fox have for me?

_____
_____
_____
_____

What is the fox asking me to be aware of?

_____
_____
_____
_____

Thoughts   Feelings

_____   _____
_____   _____
_____   _____
_____   _____

DAILY FOX MESSAGES

Fox encourages creativity

Fox Messages

Cleverness, Play & Independence are in My Day

DAILY REFLECTION

_____

_____

_____

_____

_____

_____

_____

_____

_____

_____

_____

_____

_____

_____

_____

_____

_____

_____

DAILY FOX AFFIRMATIONS

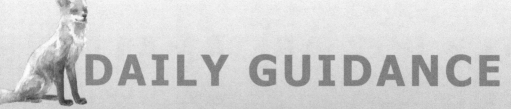

DAILY GUIDANCE

How does the fox spirit animal fit me?

_____
_____
_____
_____

What messages does the fox have for me?

_____
_____
_____
_____

What is the fox asking me to be aware of?

_____
_____
_____
_____

Thoughts	Feelings
_____	_____
_____	_____
_____	_____

DAILY FOX MESSAGES

Fox encourages creativity

Fox Messages

Cleverness, Play & Independence are in My Day

DAILY REFLECTION

DAILY FOX AFFIRMATIONS

DAILY GUIDANCE

How does the fox spirit animal fit me?

_____
_____
_____
_____

What messages does the fox have for me?

_____
_____
_____
_____

What is the fox asking me to be aware of?

_____
_____
_____
_____

Thoughts	Feelings
_____	_____
_____	_____
_____	_____
_____	_____

DAILY FOX MESSAGES

Fox encourages creativity

Fox Messages

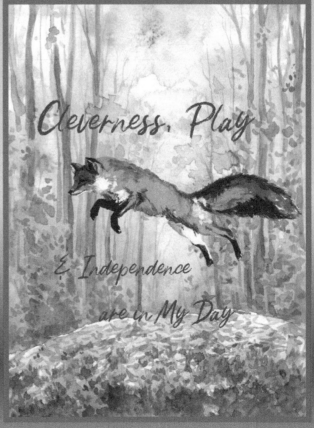

Cleverness, Play & Independence are in My Day

DAILY REFLECTION

_____
_____
_____
_____
_____
_____
_____
_____
_____
_____
_____
_____
_____
_____
_____
_____
_____
_____

DAILY FOX AFFIRMATIONS

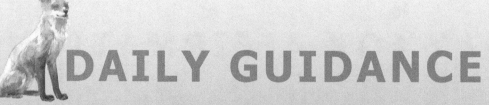

DAILY GUIDANCE

How does the fox spirit animal fit me?

_____
_____
_____
_____

What messages does the fox have for me?

_____
_____
_____
_____

What is the fox asking me to be aware of?

_____
_____
_____
_____

Thoughts   **Feelings**

_____   _____
_____   _____
_____   _____
_____   _____

DAILY FOX MESSAGES

Fox encourages creativity

Fox Messages

Cleverness, Play & Independence are in My Day

DAILY REFLECTION

_____

_____

_____

_____

_____

_____

_____

_____

_____

_____

_____

_____

_____

_____

_____

_____

DAILY FOX AFFIRMATIONS

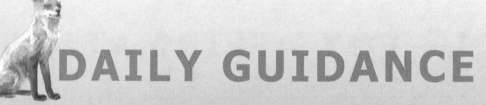

DAILY GUIDANCE

How does the fox spirit animal fit me?

_____
_____
_____
_____

What messages does the fox have for me?

_____
_____
_____
_____

What is the fox asking me to be aware of?

_____
_____
_____
_____

Thoughts	Feelings
_____	_____
_____	_____
_____	_____
_____	_____

DAILY FOX MESSAGES

Fox encourages creativity

Fox Messages

Cleverness, Play & Independence are in My Day

DAILY REFLECTION

_____
_____
_____
_____
_____
_____
_____
_____
_____
_____
_____
_____
_____
_____
_____
_____
_____
_____

DAILY FOX AFFIRMATIONS

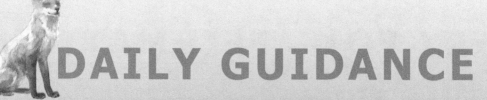

DAILY GUIDANCE

How does the fox spirit animal fit me?

_____
_____
_____
_____

What messages does the fox have for me?

_____
_____
_____
_____

What is the fox asking me to be aware of?

_____
_____
_____
_____

Thoughts   **Feelings**

_____   _____
_____   _____
_____   _____
_____   _____

DAILY FOX MESSAGES

Fox encourages creativity

Fox Messages

Cleverness, Play & Independence are in My Day

DAILY REFLECTION

DAILY FOX AFFIRMATIONS

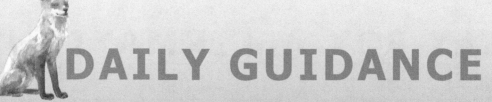

DAILY GUIDANCE

How does the fox spirit animal fit me?

_____
_____
_____
_____

What messages does the fox have for me?

_____
_____
_____
_____

What is the fox asking me to be aware of?

_____
_____
_____
_____

Thoughts   **Feelings**

_____   _____
_____   _____
_____   _____
_____   _____

DAILY FOX MESSAGES

Fox encourages creativity

Fox Messages

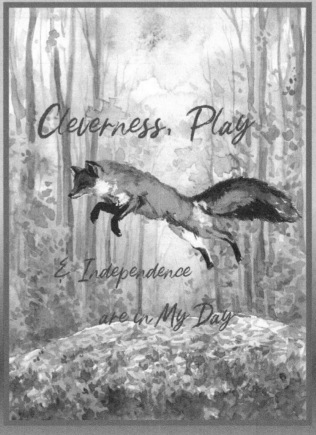

Cleverness, Play & Independence are in My Day

DAILY REFLECTION

_____
_____
_____
_____
_____
_____
_____
_____
_____
_____
_____
_____
_____
_____
_____
_____
_____
_____
_____

DAILY FOX AFFIRMATIONS

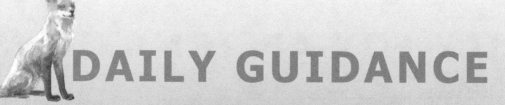

DAILY GUIDANCE

How does the fox spirit animal fit me?

_____
_____
_____
_____

What messages does the fox have for me?

_____
_____
_____
_____

What is the fox asking me to be aware of?

_____
_____
_____
_____

Thoughts

_____

_____

_____

_____

Feelings

_____

_____

_____

_____

DAILY FOX MESSAGES

Fox encourages creativity

Fox Messages

Cleverness, Play & Independence are in My Day

DAILY REFLECTION

_____
_____
_____
_____
_____
_____
_____
_____
_____
_____
_____
_____
_____
_____
_____
_____
_____

DAILY FOX AFFIRMATIONS

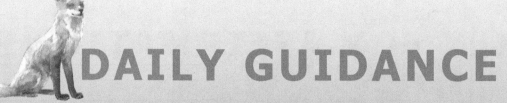

DAILY GUIDANCE

How does the fox spirit animal fit me?

_____
_____
_____
_____

What messages does the fox have for me?

_____
_____
_____
_____

What is the fox asking me to be aware of?

_____
_____
_____
_____

Thoughts   Feelings

_____   _____
_____   _____
_____   _____
_____   _____

DAILY FOX MESSAGES

Fox Messages

Fox encourages creativity

Cleverness, Play & Independence are in My Day

DAILY REFLECTION

_____
_____
_____
_____
_____
_____
_____
_____
_____
_____
_____
_____
_____
_____
_____
_____
_____

DAILY FOX AFFIRMATIONS

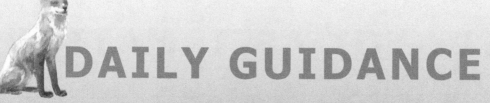

DAILY GUIDANCE

How does the fox spirit animal fit me?

_____
_____
_____
_____

What messages does the fox have for me?

_____
_____
_____
_____

What is the fox asking me to be aware of?

_____
_____
_____
_____

Thoughts	Feelings
_____	_____
_____	_____
_____	_____
_____	_____

DAILY FOX MESSAGES

Fox encourages creativity

Fox Messages

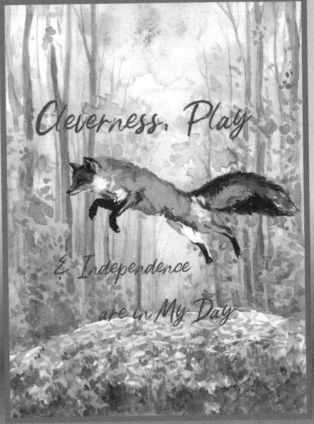

Cleverness, Play & Independence are in My Day

DAILY REFLECTION

DAILY FOX AFFIRMATIONS

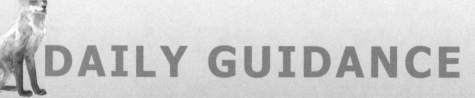

DAILY GUIDANCE

How does the fox spirit animal fit me?

_____
_____
_____
_____

What messages does the fox have for me?

_____
_____
_____
_____

What is the fox asking me to be aware of?

_____
_____
_____
_____

Thoughts   **Feelings**

_____   _____
_____   _____
_____   _____
_____   _____

DAILY FOX MESSAGES

Fox encourages creativity

Fox Messages

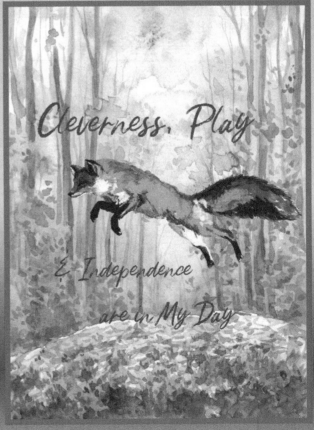

Cleverness, Play & Independence are in My Day

DAILY REFLECTION

DAILY FOX AFFIRMATIONS

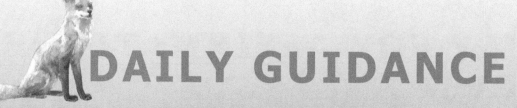

DAILY GUIDANCE

How does the fox spirit animal fit me?

_____
_____
_____
_____

What messages does the fox have for me?

_____
_____
_____
_____

What is the fox asking me to be aware of?

_____
_____
_____
_____

Thoughts   **Feelings**

_____   _____
_____   _____
_____   _____
_____   _____

DAILY FOX MESSAGES

Fox encourages creativity

Fox Messages

Cleverness, Play

& Independence

are in My Day

DAILY REFLECTION

_____
_____
_____
_____
_____
_____
_____
_____
_____
_____
_____
_____
_____
_____
_____
_____

DAILY FOX AFFIRMATIONS

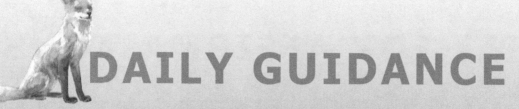

DAILY GUIDANCE

How does the fox spirit animal fit me?

_____
_____
_____
_____

What messages does the fox have for me?

_____
_____
_____
_____

What is the fox asking me to be aware of?

_____
_____
_____
_____

Thoughts   **Feelings**

_____   _____
_____   _____
_____   _____
_____   _____

DAILY FOX MESSAGES

Fox encourages creativity

Fox Messages

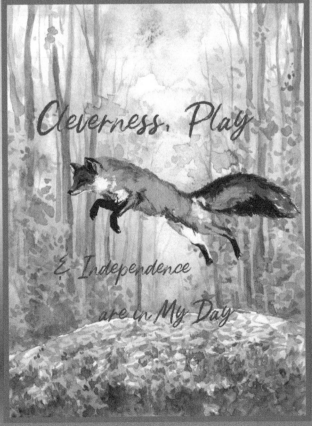

Cleverness, Play & Independence are in My Day

DAILY REFLECTION

_____
_____
_____
_____
_____
_____
_____
_____
_____
_____
_____
_____
_____
_____
_____
_____
_____
_____

DAILY FOX AFFIRMATIONS

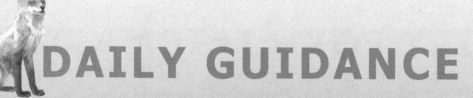

DAILY GUIDANCE

How does the fox spirit animal fit me?

_____
_____
_____
_____

What messages does the fox have for me?

_____
_____
_____
_____

What is the fox asking me to be aware of?

_____
_____
_____
_____

Thoughts   **Feelings**

_____   _____
_____   _____
_____   _____
_____   _____

DAILY FOX MESSAGES

Fox encourages creativity

Fox Messages

Cleverness, Play & Independence are in My Day

DAILY REFLECTION

_____
_____
_____
_____
_____
_____
_____
_____
_____
_____
_____
_____
_____
_____
_____
_____
_____

DAILY FOX AFFIRMATIONS

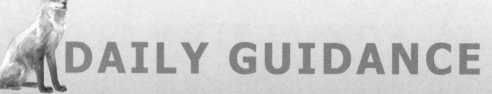

DAILY GUIDANCE

How does the fox spirit animal fit me?

_____
_____
_____
_____

What messages does the fox have for me?

_____
_____
_____
_____

What is the fox asking me to be aware of?

_____
_____
_____
_____

Thoughts   **Feelings**

_____   _____
_____   _____
_____   _____
_____   _____

DAILY FOX MESSAGES

Fox encourages creativity

Fox Messages

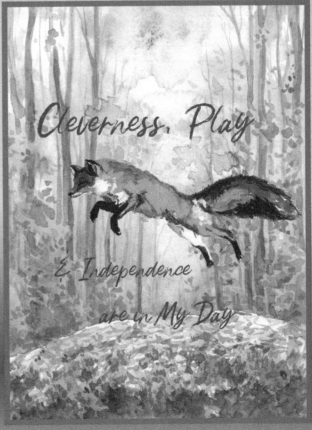

Cleverness, Play & Independence are in My Day

DAILY REFLECTION

_____
_____
_____
_____
_____
_____
_____
_____
_____
_____
_____
_____
_____
_____

DAILY FOX AFFIRMATIONS

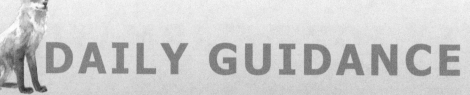

DAILY GUIDANCE

How does the fox spirit animal fit me?

_____
_____
_____
_____

What messages does the fox have for me?

_____
_____
_____
_____

What is the fox asking me to be aware of?

_____
_____
_____
_____

Thoughts   **Feelings**

_____   _____
_____   _____
_____   _____
_____   _____

DAILY FOX MESSAGES

Fox encourages creativity

Fox Messages

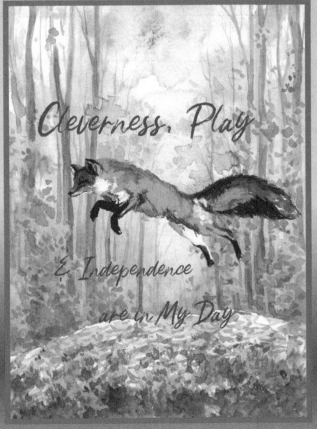

Cleverness, Play & Independence are in My Day

DAILY REFLECTION

_____
_____
_____
_____
_____
_____
_____
_____
_____
_____
_____
_____
_____
_____
_____
_____
_____
_____

DAILY FOX AFFIRMATIONS

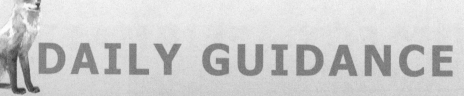

DAILY GUIDANCE

How does the fox spirit animal fit me?

_____
_____
_____
_____

What messages does the fox have for me?

_____
_____
_____
_____

What is the fox asking me to be aware of?

_____
_____
_____

Thoughts   Feelings

_____   _____
_____   _____
_____   _____

DAILY FOX MESSAGES

Fox encourages creativity

Fox Messages

Cleverness, Play & Independence are in My Day

DAILY REFLECTION

_____
_____
_____
_____
_____
_____
_____
_____
_____
_____
_____
_____
_____
_____
_____

DAILY FOX AFFIRMATIONS

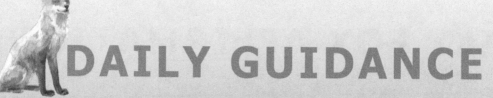

DAILY GUIDANCE

How does the fox spirit animal fit me?

_____
_____
_____
_____

What messages does the fox have for me?

_____
_____
_____
_____

What is the fox asking me to be aware of?

_____
_____
_____
_____

Thoughts   Feelings

_____   _____
_____   _____
_____   _____
_____   _____

DAILY FOX MESSAGES

Fox encourages creativity

Fox Messages

Cleverness, Play & Independence are in My Day

DAILY REFLECTION

_____
_____
_____
_____
_____
_____
_____
_____
_____
_____
_____
_____
_____
_____
_____
_____

DAILY FOX AFFIRMATIONS

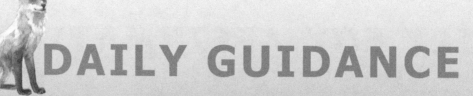

DAILY GUIDANCE

How does the fox spirit animal fit me?

_____
_____
_____
_____

What messages does the fox have for me?

_____
_____
_____
_____

What is the fox asking me to be aware of?

_____
_____
_____
_____

Thoughts   Feelings

_____   _____
_____   _____
_____   _____
_____   _____

DAILY FOX MESSAGES

Fox encourages creativity

Fox Messages

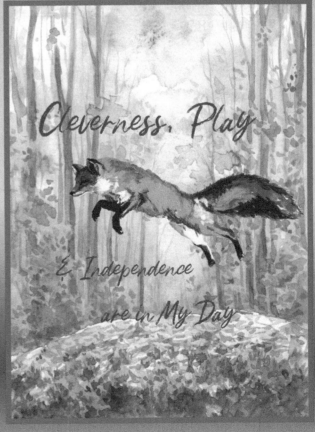

Cleverness, Play & Independence are in My Day

DAILY REFLECTION

_____
_____
_____
_____
_____
_____
_____
_____
_____
_____
_____
_____
_____
_____
_____
_____
_____

DAILY FOX AFFIRMATIONS

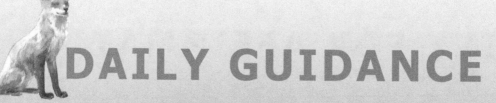

DAILY GUIDANCE

How does the fox spirit animal fit me?

_____

_____

_____

_____

What messages does the fox have for me?

_____

_____

_____

_____

What is the fox asking me to be aware of?

_____

_____

_____

_____

Thoughts   **Feelings**

_____   _____

_____   _____

_____   _____

_____   _____

DAILY FOX MESSAGES

Fox encourages creativity

Fox Messages

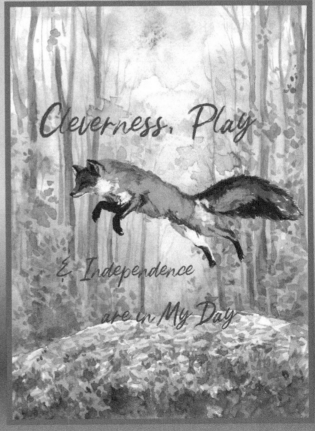

Cleverness, Play & Independence are in My Day

DAILY REFLECTION

DAILY FOX AFFIRMATIONS

DAILY GUIDANCE

How does the fox spirit animal fit me?

_____
_____
_____
_____

What messages does the fox have for me?

_____
_____
_____
_____

What is the fox asking me to be aware of?

_____
_____
_____
_____

Thoughts   **Feelings**

_____   _____
_____   _____
_____   _____

DAILY FOX MESSAGES

Fox encourages creativity

Fox Messages

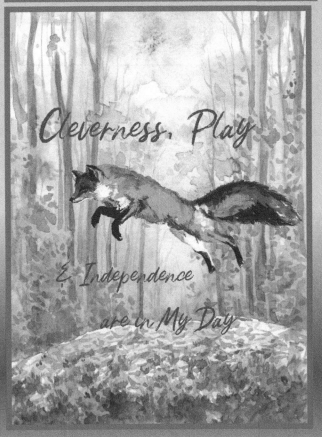

Cleverness, Play

& Independence

are in My Day

DAILY REFLECTION

_____
_____
_____
_____
_____
_____
_____
_____
_____
_____
_____
_____
_____
_____
_____
_____
_____

DAILY FOX AFFIRMATIONS

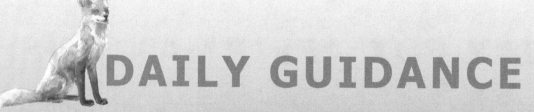

DAILY GUIDANCE

How does the fox spirit animal fit me?

_____
_____
_____
_____

What messages does the fox have for me?

_____
_____
_____
_____

What is the fox asking me to be aware of?

_____
_____
_____
_____

Thoughts   **Feelings**

_____   _____
_____   _____
_____   _____
_____   _____

DAILY FOX MESSAGES

Fox encourages creativity

Fox Messages

Cleverness, Play & Independence are in My Day

DAILY REFLECTION

DAILY FOX AFFIRMATIONS

DAILY GUIDANCE

How does the fox spirit animal fit me?

_____
_____
_____
_____

What messages does the fox have for me?

_____
_____
_____
_____

What is the fox asking me to be aware of?

_____
_____
_____
_____

Thoughts   **Feelings**

_____   _____
_____   _____
_____   _____
_____   _____

DAILY FOX MESSAGES

Fox encourages creativity

Fox Messages

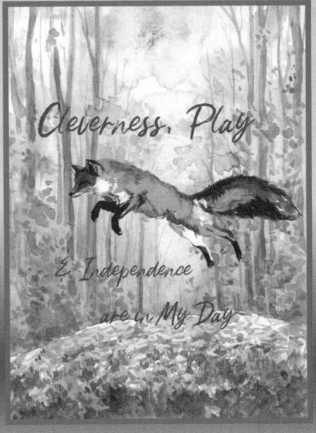

Cleverness, Play

& Independence

are in My Day

DAILY REFLECTION